WHY DIVERSITY OF EXPERIENCE
MAKES YOU A BETTER LEADER[SM]

30 Key C-suite Leadership Lessons from Each of My 5 Careers

ASH VARMA
NYC

WHY DIVERSITY OF EXPERIENCE
MAKES YOU A BETTER LEADER℠

30 Key C-suite Leadership Lessons from Each of My 5 Careers

ASH VARMA, ESQ.

Halo
PUBLISHING
INTERNATIONAL

Halo
**PUBLISHING
INTERNATIONAL**

Halo Publishing International
7550 WIH-10 #800, PMB 2069,
San Antonio, TX 78229

First Edition, November 2023
ISBN: 978-1-63765-489-7
Library of Congress Control Number: 2023916769

The information contained within this book is strictly for informational purposes.

Halo Publishing International is a self-publishing company that publishes adult fiction and non-fiction, children's literature, self-help, spiritual, and faith-based books. We continually strive to help authors reach their publishing goals and provide many different services that help them do so. We do not publish books that are deemed to be politically, religiously, or socially disrespectful, or books that are sexually provocative, including erotica. Halo reserves the right to refuse publication of any manuscript if it is deemed not to be in line with our principles. Do you have a book idea you would like us to consider publishing? Please visit www.halopublishing.com for more information.

Acknowledgements

Thank-you to all of the wonderful colleagues, leaders, friends, and clients who have been so instrumental in supporting me throughout my own growth journey. They have helped me learn and realize all the great leadership lessons that I am now able to share with you.

A special thank-you to Amy Friedman (CEO of Partners International) a wonderful colleague, friend and mentor throughout; Jerry Joyce who brought a young attorney into Media and Business; Alex Bransford who taught me much about being a gentleman and a lawyer; Girish Nadkarni who has always shared wonderful advice and guidance throughout; and so many many more (you know who you are and I am forever grateful)!

Also, Jade Gasper my wonderful Contributing Editor; Jenn Grace who first gave me the idea of publishing a book and introduced me to my great publisher, Halo Publishing (Lisa Umina and Fernanda Ramirez).

Finally, last but not least, to my lovely family who have been so helpful and have stood by me all along the way.

Thank you!

Preface

Throughout my careers over the last four decades as an executive leader, there have been a number of key issues that have continued to plague executive leadership and the ability for leaders to continue to grow. I have had the privilege and pleasure of working in various industries and have learned many lessons along the way.

Now, as an executive coach specializing in leadership development and career transition, I am seeing these same issues holding back clients from getting the careers they want or advancing in their own companies and positions.

Throughout this book, I am going to let you in on these valuable lessons, as well as some of my more vulnerable moments in learning them, with hopes that many will resonate with you and help you on your own path to passion and success. In the end, it is our experiences that shape us and help us to learn and grow, if we are willing to listen to them and reflect upon them.

Contents

WORKBOOK

WORKBOOK

Career #4
Introduction

LESSON 21

Story #21

LESSON 22

Story #22

LESSON 23

Story #23

Pre-Career

Introduction

LEADERSHIP

- Leadership and Knowledge Begin with True Empathy

- Kindness is Always its Own Reward

- Be as Inclusive as Possible

- Everyone Needs an Opportunity

- There is a Universal Language of Kindness

Pre-Career

LESSON 1

Leadership and Knowledge
Begin with True Empathy

Story #1

THE INDIAN AMERICAN EXPERIENCE, RACE RELATIONS, AND RACISM

Growing up as an Indian American in New York City in the 1960s and 1970s was an interesting experience. As the country went through major social, cultural, and historical revolutions, being Indian American (or Brown) was somewhat unique in that I was often told, "You are neither Black nor White."

For me, this was quite empowering because I was able to feel comfortable with individuals of all races, even when they were sometimes at odds during these times.

While in NYC, I never actually experienced racism personally; however, I was completely empathetic to my friends and fellow people of color who often did.

My first real experience with racism directed towards me personally did not occur until I went to England as a graduate student. There I was met with a multitude of eye-opening events. A couple of times in London, some men and women yelled at me, "F—ing Paki! Go home!" I was even chased down High Street one evening by some townies with hockey sticks. I thought they would surely kill me if they had the chance. Quite some awakening...

Yet in retrospect, I am actually glad to have had the experience to truly know what racism can feel like.

As I often traveled to adjacent countries in Europe during my student time in England, I thought about and noted how racism actually seemed to manifest itself a bit differently, starting with what specific ethnic and/or racial groups it was primarily directed against, depending upon the country I was in. I think that economics sometimes has a role to play as well.

Review of Lesson

Learned

Leadership and Knowledge Begin with True Empathy

While I obviously do not recommend getting chased down an alley with hockey sticks, I would say that truly trying to put yourself in another person's shoes is the beginning of empathy and true leadership, a lesson from which we can all certainly benefit.

Pre-Career

LESSON 2

Kindness is Always its Own Reward

Story #2

THE PORTER AND THE FARMERS' MARKET

In contrast to the racist experiences described above, during my graduate studies in the United Kingdom, I experienced many prime examples of wonderful friendship, collegiality, and education. And I want to clearly add up front that neither within the university itself nor from any university students did I ever experience any such unpleasantries.

There was one rather interesting scenario which I also found very meaningful. One morning, as I was getting ready to go to class, the porter (who happened to be a White gentleman) came to check in and look after the room, etc. My natural inclination was to ask him if he might like to have a cup of coffee, as I was in the midst of making one.

His reaction quite surprised me. He stopped short, paused, and almost with a tear in his eye said, "You know, in my twenty-plus years here, no one has ever asked me that."

Wow. I found it very humbling and was proud to share our coffees together—an educational, first-hand example of culture and class ramifications.

Later that fall, I found myself shopping one day in the farmers' market down the road. As I was looking into making a small food purchase, who but the porter should suddenly appear? He came up to the vendor I was speaking with, gave her a big hug, and said, "Now, you treat my friend here just right. You give him the best buy you can and the best price!"

I thanked him for his kind words, and we shared mutual smiles. It left a very nice feeling inside thereafter.

Review of Lesson 2
Learned

Kindness Is Always Its Own Best Reward

My lifelong mantra has always been to never under-estimate the deep healing power of a few simple kind words.

Pre-Career

LESSON 3

Be as Inclusive as Possible

Story #3

WEAVING THE GENERATIONS IN THE INDIA FESTIVAL COMMITTEE

By the time I was a college senior, because I was lucky enough to work with the New York City Department of Cultural Affairs during my student summers, I had built up a fair amount of experience conducting street festivals and fairs. Simultaneously, as the Indian American community was growing, it was my hope to help create the first-ever India Festival in Central Park.

To that end, I put together a great group of participants, spanning all ages and genders, to try to orchestrate this. With everyone's diligent efforts, we were able to successfully launch in 1974.

Through this experience as a young leader, I learned to manage meetings in which people represented several different generations, including elder generations who in the Indian American community commanded a great deal of respect.

As chairman of the India Festival Committee (IFC), what I found most helpful was having all our leadership members sit around the table together (usually with some great tea and samosas) and carefully go around the table on every major issue to make sure that everyone felt included. This was particularly important for those in the group who were a little shy about speaking up. I especially tried to make sure to ask the latter what their thoughts might be. By attempting to empower all voices, people felt heard, and we were then lucky enough to manage most major decisions with a true consensus.

Review of Lesson

Learned

Always Make Sure to Try
and Be as Inclusive as Possible

Making sure to be fully inclusive of all members in a group is an incredibly important aspect of being a better leader, and one which I have tried to follow in each of my career endeavors. Inclusion encompasses accepting and accommodating multigenerational, racial/ethnic, gender, personality, and other differences among participants and members. Make inclusion part of your efforts with everyone as much as you can.

Pre-Career

LESSON 4
Everyone Needs an Opportunity

Story #4

GROWING UP IN SPANISH HARLEM IN NYC

As I mentioned above, I grew up in NYC in the '60s and '70s, but where I grew up was also interesting. My father was a professor—a wonderful, noble career but, as we all know, typically and sadly not often an economically lucrative one.

We lived in what was then called Spanish Harlem. Honestly, this was a very rough neighborhood. As I used to tell my friends, it was "much like growing up in *West Side Story*, only without the music."

At my local grade school, we had a student who once allegedly set fire to his apartment. And in second grade, I had someone put a knife to my neck. After that, my parents were desperate to try and get us out of that school if at all possible.

Through the wonderful generosity of The Ethical Culture School, I was given a full scholarship and began attending in third grade, along with my younger sister. I am and always have been forever grateful for just being given the opportunity. (I later went on to serve on the alumni board for a good twenty-five years or so.)

If I had not been given that opportunity, using another of my favorite sayings, "There, but for the grace of God, go I."

Review of Lesson Learned

Everyone Needs to Be Given an Opportunity

This is so, so critical. We see it in our work, in our companies, in our trying to heal past grievances. Without fair opportunity, situations often cannot be bettered. Doing our best to truly try and provide opportunities does, in fact, help make the world a better place.

Pre-Career

LESSON 5

There is a Universal Language of Kindness

Story #5

WORLD TRAVEL AND THE LESSON OF LANGUAGE UNSPOKEN

As noted above, being the child of a professor, we typically did not ever have a lot of money, but there were many other wonderful benefits, including meeting the likes of Margaret Mead, Robert Merton, and others in our apartment and having the choice of a myriad of books that my father collected.

Another great benefit was that we were able to go on my dad's full-year sabbatical every seven years. Since he and my mother were originally from India, my dad tried to set it up so that we would travel through Europe for a month or so, spend the bulk of the time in India, and then return via Asia.

Experiencing diverse cultures and peoples, especially as a young child, is something I would strongly recommend whenever possible. It creates a perspective that stays with you throughout your whole life.

There were many, many wonderful experiences that I was lucky enough to have, but I will simply note one key one here regarding leadership.

When I was in my teens, we were in Athens, Greece, and we decided to go out for a quick stroll through some of the more village-type side streets. One very nice, older woman motioned to us to come over and into her open flat, which was right there on the street. We did not speak Greek, nor did she speak English. But, along with her family, she so kindly offered us tea and baklava, which was just delicious.

During this brief visit together, there were a ton of hand motions, gestures, smiles, and even though we did not speak the same language, we really did. It was the universal language of kindness.

Review of Lesson Learned

There Is a Universal Multicultural Language of Kindness, Mutual Understanding, and Respect

The lesson here, I think, is for corporate leadership. Disconnects occur not only because of verbal language barriers (although that can sometimes be the situation). They also often occur for other reasons— such as, cultural, economic, and personal differences in our communications together.

When that happens, try to go back to the universal multicultural language of kindness, mutual understanding, and respect. Take the time to be a little generous. You might be quite surprised at how often that can help us at least find the origin of the (mis)understandings that we might be having in the workplace.

WORKBOOK

PRE-CAREER LESSONS (1–5)

**Themes: Empathy, the Action of Kindness,
Inclusion, Opportunity, the Language of Kindness**

Question 1: Do you recall a key opportunity, which was given to you at any point in your life, that led you to where you are today?

_____

_____

_____

_____

_____

_____

_____

Question 2: Have you experienced similar acts of kindness in your professional career (from leadership or peers)?

_____

_____

_____

_____

_____

_____

_____

_____

_____

_____

_____

_____

Question 3: What are examples of situations in which you felt that you were particularly empathetic and/or kind, and what results do you feel transpired?

_____

_____

_____

_____

_____

_____

_____

_____

_____

_____

_____

_____

_____

Career #1

Introduction
INTERNATIONAL TAX ATTORNEY

- Think Like a Lawyer

- Don't Think Like a Lawyer

- Be as Inclusive as Possible

- Foster Entrepreneurship

- Negotiate to Win

Career #1

International Tax Attorney

LESSON 6

Think Like a Lawyer

Story #6

THINK LIKE A LAWYER

There are many possible leadership lessons that can relate to the Socratic method of teaching made popular in *The Paper Chase*. It is a rigorous method of legal teaching and learning. Having studied at Columbia University Law School, I can fairly well attest to that.

This method teaches one to think in a certain way. To succeed, it is important to think of all aspects—any area that may be questioned—and sometimes think outside the box as well.

Those of you in talent management and HR can certainly recognize the parallels here to when we utilize 360s in our executive-coaching leadership assignments. In a 360, we executive coaches interview a number of people around the coaching candidates to get a full-scale view of what others think of them, what issues they may have, what their strengths are, etc. This is a very useful tool for us in our initial analyses.

Similarly, in our C-suite business leadership areas, thinking in this way—holistically examining every aspect from every point of view—has been immensely helpful for me. As a CFO for various entities, I can think of many examples. One major one was a significant potential acquisition/merger in which the numbers all made sense, the strategy made sense, and the team that was going to lead made sense. On paper, the skills and experience of the leadership met all criteria.

But, as we looked deeper into the dynamics of one particular key leader, we realized that this person was no longer best suited for the role. This all came quite a bit out of the blue. Without that additional outside analysis, we might not have discovered this in time.

Luckily, we were able to change course fairly quickly, and no major harm was done. If we had just stuck to the usual parameters and exercises, a major opportunity might have been lost.

Review of Lesson Learned

Think Like a Lawyer

So, as a C-suite leader, it is really important to continuously review every variable in your internal analysis, especially with respect to major decisions. Think about all sides of the equation, think outside the box, and then reimagine the results with a fully open mind. This way, you can hopefully feel quite comfortable with your decision to move forward (or not).

Career #1

International Tax Attorney

LESSON 7

Don't Think Like a Lawyer

Story #7

DON'T THINK LIKE A LAWYER

In contrast to the above, sometimes as a C-suite leader, it is important to not think like a lawyer.

I remember so well when I first made the switch from being an attorney to a business CFO. I first called some of my old legal colleagues back and jokingly asked, "Uh, hey, can I have this memo...like tomorrow morning...?"

After that, so many of my business colleagues expressly mentioned the following:

> *...and stop thinking like a lawyer. We don't need all the what-ifs, all the on-the-one-hand, on-the-other-hand language, etc. Ash, what we are going to need is a decision.*

Wow. Interesting awakening, but I do believe it is quite true.

Again, I have had so many examples in which I at least tried my best to think like a lawyer when analyzing what could possibly go wrong with a path or a strategy, fully realizing that at the end of the day, we needed a decision.

Analysis paralysis is already a major problem in corporate America today, without adding any other elements.

7

Review of Lesson Learned

Don't Think Like a Lawyer

My best advice here is, do as much repostulating, thinking, and analyzing as you can, but with a very specific deadline in mind. Then make a decision! You may end up being wrong, but making no decision is actually much worse!

Career #1

International Tax Attorney

LESSON 8

Be as Inclusive as Possible

Story #8

INCLUSION AND EQUALITY
IN THE WORKPLACE

When I first joined Paul, Weiss, Rifkind, Wharton & Garrison, there were very few female partners in White-Shoe Wall Street law firms—very, very few, if any, at most of them.

Similarly, if I had to count the number of South Asian attorneys at said law firms at the time, I could honestly tabulate the total on one hand.

Thus, as a young associate, among the many things I really loved about this law firm was its major commitment to equality and diversity, even far back in its origin. The firm clearly had a strong reputation in these areas over the years, but it was actually something that the partners I primarily dealt with talked a lot about, even back in the 1980s.

I always felt comfortable in my practice there, even though I am sure I certainly must have stood out to some extent as just being different. But what matters most here is how people were made to feel. And I know, for me, I definitely felt included, even if I was clearly a minority of one.

While I was there, many new women partners were promoted again adding to the firm's expressed commitments. (I have also been a lifelong advocate for women leaders and entrepreneurs.)

In essence, as I think might be clear from the above, when an entity does or at least attempts to do the right things and openly communicates the same, it can create long-lasting goodwill among its employees.

Review of Lesson

Learned

Always Make Sure to Try and Be as Inclusive as Possible and Communicate Well and Often

Making sure to be fully inclusive of all members is an important aspect of a company's well-being, and it makes its leaders even stronger. Not only is it the right thing to do, but it can also have long-lasting dividends well into the future. Be sure to never lose sight of this.

Career #1

International Tax Attorney

Story #9

CELEBRATING OPPORTUNITIES THROUGH ENTREPRENEURSHIP

In my own personal story, I ended up working for almost two years on an incredible assignment with an amazing entrepreneur, after which I was asked to join him as his CFO.

Rather than taking the view that I was no longer a part of the Paul, Weiss, Rifkind, Wharton & Garrison family, the firm instead fostered and assisted the growing relationship. For me, this was so important since who knew whether my client could actually pull off the first major media Leveraged Buy Out.

The firm absolutely took the supportive view, which again I must say is such a wise view to take but is not often the case.

Moreover, I had several colleagues I knew at the firm who later and similarly moved on to various entrepreneurial ventures. So, it was definitely a strong practice there to help nourish and assist since, as we know from Lesson #6 and Lesson #7, lawyers may (or may not) make the best C-suite business executives.

Thus, encouraging and fostering an entrepreneurial environment is a really good thing to do. General Electric (GE) was quite famous for doing the same in its various business units, often with some of its key C-suite business leaders. (See, for example, the article about how GE fostered internal entrepreneurship.)[1]

In my own experience at several different entities for which I worked, we too from time to time would find very promising employees who felt the need to do it on their own and make their own place for themselves. Rather than feeling hurt at the potential for abandonment, it is so much better to help, assist, and nourish their dreams and hopes, even if you know that they may someday leave.

Again, it is a good lesson to learn to assist in these scenarios and not penalize employees or close down, as others have sometimes done in the past.

[1] Dryfoos, R. (2017, November 15). Make Innovation Part of Everyone's Job—How Cisco, GE, Adobe, and Intuit Do Intrapreneurship. Innov8rs. https://innov8rs.co/news/make-innovation-part-every-ones-job-cisco-ge-adobe-intuit-intrapreneurship/.

Review of Lesson Learned

Foster Entrepreneurship and Other Endeavors Your Employees May Choose to Follow, Even If They Will One Day Leave You

When your employees decide to think about things in a different way, move in a different direction, or even move on altogether, try to nurture and assist, rather than be an impediment. You should really try to think about their future successes elsewhere as a testament to what they learned and what you provided them. So, yes, it is a loss, but not really—if you try and think about it that way.

Career #1

International
Tax Attorney

LESSON 10

Negotiate to Win

Story #10

THE ULTIMATE NEGOTIATORS & KEEPING THINGS IN BALANCE

A perhaps unspoken tact in the legal lexicon is that on a case or during a negotiation, the key is often to win as much as you can for your client(s). That is how they typically measure you and what they are looking for. The more you can gain for your clients, the better.

However, I do want to note one small caveat here which I personally witnessed. There was a substantial negotiation that was taking place regarding a potential large acquisition. The parties were such that one had quite a lot of leverage. They (and their lawyers) kept hammering point after point, issue after issue, over the course of many months. The end result was that they basically won every major point.

On the one hand, this seemed like a great victory, and much celebration ensued. However, once the acquisition was completed, another story emerged.

In most major acquisitions, there are many variables and a fair amount of transitioning that must occur. How cooperative do you think the acquired party was in said transition, having been beaten up so badly during negotiations?

Yes, you guessed it. Not very.

I would have to say that in the end I am not sure that the winning party didn't in some respects lose more (money and goodwill), by taking such a win-at-all-costs strategy, than they would have if they hadn't had to win every single major point.

Food for thought…sometimes the greatest victories can be somewhat Pyrrhic in retrospect.

10

Review of Lesson Learned

Negotiate to Win, but Be Careful of Winning Everything!

Negotiate as hard as you can. Win the most major points. But be a bit careful of winning every major negotiating point. The total victory may come back to bite you in the future.

WORKBOOK

CAREER #1 LESSONS (6–10)

Themes: Analysis, Decisiveness, Inclusivity, Entrepreneurship, Negotiation Balance

Question 1: Do you recall a situation in which you or your leader got stuck in analysis paralysis and therefore missed a key opportunity? How was it handled? How do you feel it could have been handled better?

_____

_____

_____

_____

_____

_____

Question 2: When decision-making, time is key. What methods do you typically use in your own decision-making? Gut instinct, research, others' input? Think of a problem or opportunity that currently exists in your workplace. How will you tackle it? Have you tried a pros-cons and a resources-needed list?

_____

_____

_____

_____

_____

_____

_____

_____

_____

_____

_____

_____

Question 3: We all like to win. How can we win and keep a balance? Are you bringing others into the conversation? What are some ideas for how you and your leadership can help integrate others into the process?

_____

_____

_____

_____

_____

_____

_____

_____

_____

_____

_____

_____

Career #2

Introduction
CFO of the World's Largest Billboard Company

- Be Your True, Authentic Self

- Kindness is NOT the Same as Weakness

- Don't Be Afraid to Think Totally "Outside the Box"

- Overcome Silos & Underappreciation

- Have Courage & Confidence

Career #2

CFO of the World's Largest Billboard Company

LESSON 11

Be Your True, Authentic Self

Story #11

ESTABLISHING RELATIONSHIPS THROUGH TRANSPARENCY AND AUTHENTICITY

As many of you know, two of the most valued traits most people seek in a leader these days are transparency and authenticity. People want to know that the person who is leading the company and/or their area(s) is genuine. When they feel that the person has a hidden agenda, or if the person is not relatable, there is quite often a huge disconnect.

Another key variable I suggest is that establishing your authenticity as a leader starts with establishing the relationships and the rapport in a way that conveys that you are an actual real human being too.

So many times, I hear that employees have no real connection to their C-suite leaders, view them much as suits, and oftentimes feel that said C-suite leaders don't show them much to dissuade them from thinking this way.

Add to that, when it comes to environments such as Wall Street and/or finance, many rank-and-file employees have a healthy dose of skepticism in their initial dealings with leaders. This is an area I focus very intently on with many of my executive-coaching clients who are making a shift from corporate America to running their own entrepreneurial ventures.

I had an interesting experience when first joining a major media company some years back. The new owners were considered Northerners, and in my case, this was compounded by the fact that I was coming in from NYC with a Wall Street perception (although not really). Plus, I am certain that I was the only person of color in a senior C-suite leadership position at that time in the industry.

Our initial meetings about budgets, details, strategies, and creating relationships were cordial. But what was really wonderful was that we had planned a several-day, off-site event, with all the key branch and division leaders, to get to know one another better.

Things had been going quite well, and on the last evening, not really planned, there was a dinner with background music.

Now, those of you who know me well know that I really love to dance...being a CFO and all...but really.

So, what ended up happening that evening was that slowly a few of us, and soon nearly all of us, started to get up, dance, and enjoy the camaraderie in a really lovely way.

In my case, truth be told, I was probably (as usual) one of the last ones to leave the dance floor.

My boss took me aside later and said to me, "You gained more trust and more goodwill than you can imagine, just by being yourself and showing everyone that you are a real person and not just a suit."

Now, of course, that wasn't why I did it, but the effect was really wonderful to see. The next day, I saw a number of smiling faces in the meetings. Not that there weren't any before, there were just more. :)

11

Review of Lesson Learned

Be Your True, Authentic Self

Now, of course, I am not saying that you need to plan to and/or should always get up on the dance floor, but I am saying that as a C-suite leader, you should not be afraid to show your true, authentic self to your employees. It is so valuable when your employees can feel that, in some respects at least, you are just another human being like them, trying your best to help move the company forward. Try it and see the value therein.

Career #2

CFO of the World's Largest Billboard Company

LESSON 12
Kindness is NOT the Same as Weakness

Story #12

BE HUMAN. BE KIND. BE FIRM.

In contrast to the above, sometimes many C-suite leaders fear that if they show too much of themselves— their humanism, their kindness—it can sometimes backfire on them. The view is that people won't respect the decisions, particularly the hard ones, that we know we all have to make from time to time as C-suite leaders.

While there is certainly some merit to this worry, in my own experience I would say that if you try to balance the two correctly, it need not backfire at all. In fact, it can create a really healthy working relationship on both fronts.

Here is another example from my own C-suite leadership learnings, which I think demonstrates this.

In this particular case, I was down in one of our company's Deep South divisions for a three-day stretch. We were in the midst of some detailed budget-review meetings that seemed to have gone quite well, with open discussions and plenty of positive give-and-take.

However, as the CFO of this entity, I had to make some final financial decisions. There was one area in which the division made a good argument for additional capital expenditures, but it really wasn't the best way for the company to go at that time and place. I ultimately told them no and explained why.

That evening, we all had a wonderful dinner together (no dancing this time) and spent more time getting to know one another better. Everyone clearly had a great time together.

The next day, the divisional head and the accounting manager came to see me. Although the Capital Expenditures decision was final, they tried to revisit it again—with a lot of smiles—courtesy, I am sure, of the prior evening's dinner.

I listened carefully, took stock of the situation, and said, "This wasn't in the budget yesterday. I really had a wonderful time getting to know you all better last evening, but it wasn't in the budget yesterday, and it's still not in the budget today." Simple and straightforward. They both kind of looked at one another, smiled again, and we moved on together from there.

You can really enjoy the company of your colleagues and employees, but a financial decision does not change based on that.

12

Review of Lesson Learned

Kindness is NOT the Same as Weakness

Building relationships and being kind is its own best reward. However, that doesn't mean that if it wasn't in the budget yesterday, it is now going to suddenly be in the budget today simply because we have built up a nice camaraderie. Keeping the two separate and distinct is certainly difficult at times, but I suggest it is eminently doable as a key C-suite leadership practice.

Career #2

CFO of the World's Largest Billboard Company

LESSON 13

Don't Be Afraid to Think Totally "Outside the Box"

Story #13

FINDING NEW AND UNUSUAL SOLUTIONS

Another key C-suite leadership practice that employees are looking for is thinking outside the box, meaning new and innovative ideas when the circumstances call for it. This trait is also highly valued in numerous studies that have been done, and certainly speaks for itself.

One example I had the good fortune of being involved in was with another media company at a later stage of my career. Here, the company had the chance to create a marketing bonanza for its owners and itself. It had a unique media opportunity with some prime properties that were really valuable. At the same time, it also had some more laggard properties that had not typically been so marketable in the more recent past.

With the help of a media-engineering expert, we reconfigured our entire inventory. We created circles of opportunity and then put together a detailed buying program: if clients wanted some of our most valued properties, they had to purchase additional incremental amounts of some of our other more laggard ones. This ended up becoming a long-term strategic solution and solidified the base and the value. The company was quite successful in this endeavor.

So sometimes just thinking of something new and innovative can really help. The teamwork created through selling these newly constructed opportunities was also infectious, as one might imagine, which was a wonderful by-product of creative innovation.

Don't be afraid to do something totally new—something that has never been done before. If well thought out, the dividends can be extremely meaningful.

13

Review of Lesson Learned

Don't Be Afraid to Think Totally "Outside the Box" and Try Something New—The Results May Surprise You

Being innovative is a strong trait for C-suite leaders. It can not only create tremendous business and financial value, but also sometimes totally reenergize your employees and colleagues as a nice by-product.

Career #2

CFO of the World's Largest Billboard Company

LESSON 14
Overcome Silos and Underappreciation

Story #14

OVERCOMING SILOS & UNDERAPPRECIATION

I have talked elsewhere in more depth about the problem of silos in corporate America (see *Inc.com* article "How to Eliminate the Age-Old Conflict Between Sales and Accounting").[2]

When people don't talk to one another, when they don't even understand the value that their fellow employees and colleagues can bring, this is a huge problem. People are left in their own particular silos and don't get to interact as much as needed for future growth.

Even though I had to deal with this a few times in my prior C-suite endeavors, I am a bit saddened to say that in my current role as an executive leadership coach, I hear and see that this still remains a huge problem in much of corporate America today.

---

[2] Haden, J. (2013, January 11). *How to eliminate the age-old conflict between sales & accounting—Inc.com. Inc.com*. https://www.inc.com/jeff-haden/how-to-eliminate-the-age-old-conflict-between-sales-and-accounting-fri.html.

Besides the obvious lost production value, employee relationships also keenly suffer in the process. Silos don't create the proper environment for those relationships to grow, and don't allow employees to take the company even further together.

Without a basic understanding of your colleagues' worth and value, siloing can only make it worse.

In the more detailed piece cited above, I give a much fuller analysis, but I will simply summarize some of the key highlights here regarding one major example that I had to deal with and solve.

In a nutshell, this company's sales and marketing department had essentially stopped talking to the accounting department, and vice versa. The departments were on different floors, and you could see that the sense of mutual respect had been deeply eroded over time.

I came in on a brand-new leadership basis, and within a week I could see the problem. I immediately called an all-hands meeting and sat down with everyone involved, all together in a large conference room. I began by talking about what sales and marketing thought of accounting (a bunch of pencil pushers, always creating roadblocks, etc.) and then about what accounting thought of sales and marketing (a bunch of prima donnas, never following rules, etc.).

Then I startled everyone by saying, "Well, you are both right to some extent. But you need to try and understand the roles in terms of what each group is trying to do, the obstacles they face in doing so, and why each of you thinks what you seem to think."

Then, most importantly, I walked through a full six-step process as to why and how each group was critical to the functioning of the company. I helped them see their roles in creating the company's full value. And most importantly to them, I explained that if they didn't cooperate with one another, in the end no one could get paid.

That certainly caught their attention.

I then told them that they needed to work together better—much, much better—and am happy to say that things began to change almost immediately. In fact, we then went on to increase operating cash flow by nearly 100 percent in only eighteen months.

Silos, underappreciation of colleagues, and misunderstandings about what employees actually do and why they do it are often the leading causes of huge disconnects in corporate America. These are issues that we, as key C-suite leaders, need to be fully aware of and mitigate to the best of our ability.

Review of Lesson Learned

Overcome Silos and Underappreciation. Corporate Silos, Underappreciation of Colleagues, and Misunderstandings about the Value of Colleagues Are Issues to Always Try to Mitigate as Soon as Possible

Building collegiality begins with at least having an understanding about what your fellow colleagues do and why their work is valuable. Then, even if you might not like some of those components, there must be mutual respect and absolute cooperation. Key roles for the C-suite leader are to always be on the lookout for these problems and then solve them as quickly as possible should they unfortunately arise.

Career #2

CFO of the World's Largest Billboard Company

LESSON 15
Have Courage & Confidence

Story #15

BE COURAGEOUS & CONFIDENT IN DECISION-MAKING

Another (of the many) key C-suite leadership traits is courage.

There will be times when tough decisions have to be made—sometimes, ones that can have a major impact on many.

One should never—never ever—be cavalier here. Always think through to the best of your ability all key options. And if something is unpleasant, consider whether and how it might be avoided.

Still, in some instances, the hard decisions will have to be made. Although I am lucky enough in my C-suite experience to have countless stories of growth, advancement, progress, and joy, I also have stories of painful downsizings, having to let people go, etc.

I always suggest that kindness and communication are key in the latter cases. Be straightforward. Don't sugarcoat, but be appreciative and real. In the end, even if people are unhappy with the outcome, they will respect authenticity.

One example where I had to attempt to be particularly courageous is the following: After much deliberation, we decided that a certain executive had to be let go. Under the circumstances, the facts spoke for themselves.

As the C-suite leader, I took on the responsibility of having the conversation with the executive. In and of itself, there was nothing particularly different here. But the unusual part was that many of us knew that this individual had a firearm permit and carried a firearm in the glove compartment of his car.

I had a very rational discussion with the individual. The person was upset, but could see a little bit of the why. I then had the person escorted out by some key individuals my team had decided on together. We hoped for no additional repercussions, and luckily there weren't any. But it certainly did give us all a bit of pause.

Hopefully, none of you will ever have to face a similar situation. But the key remains: think things through carefully, and try for other solutions. If there aren't any, then follow through. But plan and be prepared for any other contingencies.

Review of Lesson Learned

Have Courage and Confidence in the Face of Difficult Decisions

Sometimes we all have to make some difficult decisions. If you have properly thought them through, then be sure to have the courage to do what you feel you must. But always, as well, prepare for any other possible difficult outcomes.

WORKBOOK

CAREER #2 LESSONS (11–15)

Themes: Authenticity, Kindness, Innovation, Appreciation, Courage

Question 1: When you have been involved in—or have been affected by -- a major corporate change or restructuring, did you feel that your senior leadership communicated the situation appropriately? What would you have done differently?

_____

_____

_____

_____

_____

_____

Question 2: Can you think of any situations in which thinking out of the box would have provided a better and potentially faster solution?

_____

_____

_____

_____

_____

_____

_____

_____

_____

_____

_____

_____

_____

Question 3: Have you yourself, or others in your company, experienced being siloed off and not being valued as key additional participants? If so, how would you have provided for more inclusiveness?

_____

_____

_____

_____

_____

_____

_____

_____

_____

_____

_____

_____

Career #3

Introduction

Entrepreneur & Consultant

- Don't Be Afraid to Look at Things in a New Way
- Consolidate Your Strategy and Communicate Together
- Don't Be Afraid to Create Something Totally New
- Know Your Audience and Adapt
- Try to Manage "The Big" with "The Small"

Career #3

Entrepreneur & Consultant

LESSON 16
Don't Be Afraid to Look at Things in a New Way

Story #16

RETHINK YOUR CORE PRODUCTS AND BUSINESS

As a consultant and entrepreneur, many clients look to you to help them solve problems of many sorts. As a former financial CFO, I have often been involved with providing strategic advice to many of my clients, regarding raising new monies, reconfiguring business plans, growth, and mergers and acquisitions.

Of course, each client and each situation is different, but here is where a broad diversity of experience can often be very helpful. There are numerous examples I could reference, but I will start with one that was particularly interesting.

The assignment was to work with an international company that was looking to grow and raise additional monies. The senior management team consisted of primarily tech and engineering experts. Their products were great, but their perspective was always that of manufacturing.

With my extensive media background, I was able to see that the company's products were actually, at their essence, wonderful vehicles for media and communications as well. I explained to the team that if they were able to be considered a successful media company, their valuations would be much higher.

We thus began extensive work together, reconfiguring what the company's core products were and what vehicles they were utilizing. Then we put together a business presentation for a major international bank.

Ultimately, the company was not only able to successfully raise the funding it sought, but they even won a major award at the bank for most innovative and creative new business plan.

So, what is the key lesson here regarding C-suite leadership? It is to not be afraid to see through a different lens when analyzing your core company's expertise and products. Reconfiguring and retransforming can often prove very helpful.

16

Review of Lesson Learned

Don't Be Afraid to Look at Things in a New Way

Often, we operate from the perspective of our prior knowledge and can only see through the lens of our own experiences. Sometimes, however, bringing in a whole new idea and looking through a new lens is not only beneficial in general, but it may in fact result in higher financial valuations. Always keep an open mind.

Career #3

Entrepreneur
& Consultant

LESSON 17

*Consolidate Your Strategy
and Communicate Together*

Story #17

START WITH ONE KEY EXPERTISE
& THEN EXPAND

As a consultant, I have witnessed and worked with many companies that are really good at a couple of things, but either can't figure out where to start or try to start everything at once.

Now, there are, of course, always exceptions to the rule, but in my own experience, I have seen that trying to be all things to all people is usually not the winning course. One such example is a major media company that I consulted with as a strategic financial advisor.

The company was actually trying to go down three separate media paths simultaneously, each with its own senior leadership and beginning infrastructure. On their own, each path might have had a reasonable chance at success, but without focus on one primary initiative, the company was being torn apart. This was compounded by the fact that the key senior leaders were often working independently and not effectively communicating with one another.

So the first thing I had to work on was just getting the senior leaders to talk to one another. Truth be told, sometimes I had to actually function more like a go-between.

Next, I was finally able to get the senior leaders to agree on the most likely beginning strategic approach. Here, I was able to help them create their projections, which was actually kind of fun since it included some very talented and creative media people who really hadn't worked in the financial realm before.

With a detailed financial plan in place (totally built from the bottom up), the company was able to get the funding it sought.

The lessons in this story are that, first, it really is not a good idea to try to do all things at once. Be the master of a specialty, build your expertise, and expand from there. (I often call this the Walt Disney model.) Next, communication is key. You have got to talk to one another, even if it sometimes means bringing in an outsider to help accomplish that.

Review of Lesson Learned

Consolidate Your Strategy and Communicate Together!

Trying to go down multiple paths at once is usually not the best way for a company to succeed. Figure out what your core, essential, best-played strategy is and start from there. Then, as you are successful in that initial arena, growth and financial investment becomes much more likely.

Additionally, communicate more effectively among the senior leadership team. If you absolutely cannot mitigate the issues with senior leadership, bring in a trusted third party to help mediate the communication process. Without doing so, sustainable progress won't be made.

Career #3

Entrepreneur & Consultant

LESSON 18

*Don't Be Afraid to Create
Something Totally New*

Story #18

DON'T BE AFRAID TO CREATE SOMETHING THAT HAS NEVER BEEN DONE BEFORE

Coming from the entrepreneurial consulting side, another key lesson for good C-suite leadership is to sometimes allow yourself to dream big and create something new. Of course, it is important to monitor those dreams with financial realities and good strategies, but starting with the "Big Dream" is also necessary.

As we know, there will always be some (sometimes many) naysayers. But dreaming and then creating something totally new can potentially pay enormous dividends.

I have many examples that I could cite here, but one of my favorites is the following: I was working as a strategic financial consultant for a former NHL player who had a dream of creating rotating poster panel advertising in professional arenas. It would allow companies to buy all the sports signage around the arena, instead of only purchasing single-sign locations, as was common at the time.

In the context of NHL games, the poster signage had to be technologically created to allow for a "true bounce" because a puck might hit it. This, they accomplished.

In terms of marketing and brand exposure, the company created a full outdoor-skating arena in Las Vegas, behind Caesar's Palace, where the NY Rangers and LA Kings (including the legendary Wayne Gretzky) flew in to play a promotional game to highlight the new technology and signage.

It was really an incredible event, despite the fact that we were told the night before that there was a good chance of rain, which usually didn't occur at that time in Las Vegas. Thankfully, it didn't come to pass! The event was an incredible success and provided much-needed exposure and business progression.

The company was later able to provide its technology and signage to many major arenas, and its impact can be seen in many more today.

So here was a completely brand-new way of looking at sports signage, a system that had to be created essentially from scratch, but it all started with one person's great vision.

Similarly, it is important for C-suite leaders to have an open mind with creative innovation, develop a vision, and always consider the ideas of their colleagues.

18

Review of Lesson Learned

Don't Be Afraid to Create Something Totally New

Sometimes it is good to just dream big and try to do something that has never been done before. Initially, many will say no, but with diligence and proper strategy, occasionally amazing results can be achieved. I always encourage new thinking. And we, as C-suite leaders, should definitely encourage this in our colleagues and employees.

Career #3

Entrepreneur & Consultant

LESSON 19

Know Your Audience and Adapt

Story #19

BASED ON YOUR AUDIENCE, CHANGE YOUR APPROACH

People have various work styes and ways of approaching things. While it is always important to be authentic, it is also important to consider that different groups may have cultures and work styles that vary from yours. This should be relatively clear, especially when dealing with international entities. However, sometimes it can also apply to styles of approach in meetings in which people come from relatively similar backgrounds.

What do I mean by this? One great example I often cite is a particular project in which my colleague and I were going to a technology company to show how they could best raise funds for its promising new products.

My colleague was from marketing and had been quite successful by often being bold in presentations and insights. This was often well received by some clients, but we worried as to whether that was quite suitable for the group in this scenario.

Within a short time in our meeting, I could see that my colleague's approach was not working. The potential client wasn't able to distill the intended message, and the boldness was not being well received.

I quickly pulled my colleague aside, talked about what was working and what was not, and then came back to move the conversation forward in a different direction that I hoped would be more effective. My colleague was also able to quickly adapt and completely shift their approach.

We were able to then stay on for another full day of meetings and ended up working together very productively with this new client.

Again, the lesson here for good C-suite leadership is to be sure to read your audience and adapt as needed. Culturally and internationally, differences are somewhat obvious. However, even within the same culture, approaches can vary. One approach might work with some, but not with others. In these cases, shift and adapt immediately. Building that relationship—and in the right way—is so very valuable.

Review of Lesson Learned

Know Your Audience and Adapt

Building relationships starts with trying to understand cultural and sometimes international differences that may be applicable. Beyond that, when an approach (which might have otherwise been successful) is not working, don't be afraid to change your approach and move forward in a better way. Building the relationship right from the start and in the right way is always key.

Career #3

Entrepreneur & Consultant

LESSON 20

Balancing Big & Small

Story #20

MANAGE "THE BIG" WITH "THE SMALL"

As a consultant/entrepreneur, I previously spoke about "The Emotional Pitfalls of Starting a Consulting Business."[3] In it, I describe what I call "having to always manage 'The Big' with 'The Small.'"

In other words, consultants often don't know from where their clients will be coming. Thus, they must spread the net wide and far — "The Big." At the same time, they will be hired for their specific expertise, not just for knowing a number of different things in general — "The Small."

Balancing big and small in proper proportion can be exhausting, but such is the case in consulting, as I have often talked about in various presentations. This is often also applicable with C-suite leaders who may not be seeking a wide variety of clients (although they could be). Some examples could include managing major corporate strategy, but without losing your core focus;

[3] Haden, J. (2014, September 15). "Starting a Consulting Business: The Emotional Pitfalls No One Talks About." Inc.com. html https://www.inc.com/jeff-haden/starting-a-consulting-business-the-emotional-pitfalls-no-one-talks-about.html.

expanding into new product lines, but making sure that the underlying production is not compromised, etc.

So for growth to occur, a good C-suite leader needs to always be thinking of new things, new ways, new approaches. However, it is critical to not lose sight of what brought the company to where it is and what has made it successful. An area in which this often occurs is in the context of a new major merger or acquisition where some of the company's key core focus is often lost.

Review of Lesson Learned

Try to Manage "The Big" with "The Small"

A good C-suite leader needs to be focused on trying to achieve balance by simultaneously managing "The Big" with "The Small." Growth needs to occur, and new avenues need to be explored, but in that process, don't lose sight of your core products and values.

WORKBOOK

CAREER #3 LESSONS (16–20)

Themes: Creative Vision, Expertise, Imagination, Culture, Balance

Question 1: Have you ever been involved in a company or company project in which too many things were trying to be accomplished at once? If so, how was this remedied, or what would you have done differently?

_____

_____

_____

_____

_____

_____

Question 2: What are some examples in which you think senior leadership should have adapted a broader vision? Why didn't they do so, and what process would you have done instead?

_____

_____

_____

_____

_____

_____

_____

_____

_____

_____

_____

_____

Question 3: Have you ever experienced a situation in which different players/stakeholders were not able to effectively communicate with one another due to cultural differences? How was that solved, and if it wasn't, what would you have done differently?

Career #4

Introduction
COO/DEI

- Speak the Language of the CFO

- Kill Them with Kindness

- Be Patient With Cultural Disconnects

- Include DEI/HR Senior Executives in Financial Decision-Making

- Support Your Middle Managers

Career #4

COO/DEI

LESSON 21

DEI Is an Investment, Not an Expense

Story #21

CFO CONSIDERATIONS ALWAYS APPLY

I first entered the field of talent management and diversity & inclusion in early 2010. In terms of D&I (now typically known as DEI), there were so many of us who were committed to the concepts and to trying to make things better for everyone. The moral imperative was always present: it is just the right thing to do.

However (and particularly as a CFO myself), I told all my colleagues that even though there is such a strong moral imperative, unfortunately, as I saw it, nothing much is going to happen until "we speak the language of the CFO!"

What did I mean by that? Primarily metrics, facts, and data. Otherwise, without the same, most typical CFOs were still going to view D&I as an expense, not as an investment.

Unfortunately, such data and metrics were not in great abundance in 2010/2011, and the results therefore reflected that.

I am so happy to see that now there are wonderful studies and metrics (see, for example, the seminal McKinsey 2020 study showing that companies are 25 percent more likely to show above-average profitability with gender diversity, and 36 percent more likely to show above-average profitability with racial and ethnic diversity!).[4]

So, thankfully, we have now entered a much better phase with truly significant investments in DEI initiatives being made by numerous companies. Hopefully they will continue. However, while wearing my CFO hat, I sometimes still caution many of my colleagues that when the bottom lines start to get affected, those investments might be among the first to be cut.

[4] Dixon-Fyle, S., Dolan, K., Hunt, D. V., & Prince, S. (2020, May 19). Diversity wins: How inclusion matters. McKinsey & Company. https://www.mckinsey.com/featured-insights/diversity-and-inclusion/diversity-wins-how-inclusion-matters.

21
Review of Lesson Learned

Speak the Language of the CFO

No matter how sound an expenditure may seem, and even be based on the highest moral ground, until you convince the CFO that it is an investment, as opposed to an expense, it will more than likely not be made. And what is necessary to convince the CFO? Data, data, data, and metrics! Always.

Career #4

COO/DEI

LESSON 22

Kill Them with Kindness

Story #22

BE PERSISTENT BUT KIND

Another very interesting experience I had in the DEI space relates to collecting a major bill. The work had been performed, all was well, and the client was quite happy.

When we sent the bill, it took some time because it first had to be routed to the European corporate office for approval. We were patient.

Then, as it was going to be approved/paid, we were told that it had to go to India for operational logistics. Now, this was delaying our payment by many months.

Although we were all clearly annoyed, I purposely never showed that. In fact, our key US contact was continually apologetic, but they really couldn't do much.

When it got stuck in India, unbelievably (well, really not in those days), it got re-sent to their European headquarters. New people, all new explanations, etc. We were approaching a year of not receiving our payment.

Again, as much as we wanted to scream, I always kept cool and polite. But every two to three weeks, I restarted all the conversations and, of course as an attorney as well, documented everything via email.

Finally, finally then, probably eighteen months or so after inception, we received our payment.

Again, so many of my team were totally frustrated, but I cautioned that continually being polite and never losing one's temper is still, in my humble opinion, the best and only way to go.

We kept the relationship intact (in fact, we got more business), but it was sometimes trying.

As my boss said to me at the end, "I see what you do here. Just kill them with kindness."

I said yes, but that also means never ever giving up!

22

Review of Lesson Learned

Kill Them with Kindness

Sometimes, we all face those trying situations that make no sense and are a cause of continual frustration. I know that there may be a time and a place to take the yelling route. However, in over thirty years of C-suite work, I still find that remaining calm, patient, and treating those on the other side with respect and kindness is still the best and most successful way to end up with what you are actually seeking.

Career #4

COO/DEI

LESSON 23
Be Patient with Cultural Disconnects

Story #23

CULTURAL EXPERIENCES
IN DECISION-MAKING

In my DEI and talent management work, I was often able to work very closely with major European entities that had substantial operations in the United States.

The DEI assignments typically focused on training, management leadership, unconscious bias, allyship, ERG/BRGs, etc. These were generally very rewarding assignments.

One thing I found very interesting, however, was there often appeared to be a bit of a disconnect between what was actually happening in the US operations versus the view of the corporate executives from Europe.

A lot of this, I think, comes from the fact that many times European countries are not typically quite as diverse as we are here in the US, especially with respect to multiracial and multicultural dimensions (though that, too, seems to be changing).

So, I think one has to allow room for a person's point of view and perception—which is often based on what they know and what they have actually experienced. In fact, if an individual hasn't seen a certain phenomenon as much as others may have (sometimes on a daily basis), they might not be as much in tune with it as the others are.

In such cases, rather than be frustrated by the apparent lack of recognition of the phenomenon being described or the appreciation of its nuances, I suggest we first start as good C-suite leaders. We do this by learning where our audience (in this case, high-ranking C-suite corporate execs themselves) may be coming from. Then we need to try to show them the differences, the situations, and the causes of what might at first seem quite foreign to them.

Only then, by educating them to some extent, will there be any chance of real progress. In other words, don't get mad—teach, help, and explain.

23

Review of Lesson Learned

Be Patient with Cultural Disconnects

Sometimes it can be very frustrating to note that what is apparent to almost everyone regarding a situation may be totally foreign to others. When this happens, misunderstandings are exacerbated, especially if the "others" are corporate C-suite leaders. In this scenario, I suggest that since they may not have seen it as much in their own corporate cultures, we should take the time, with patience and understanding, to teach and communicate what the issues are. In doing so, this will effect real and significant change in the future. It is a good C-suite leadership lesson to always keep in mind.

Career #4

COO/DEI

LESSON 24

Increased Engagement

Story #24

OPENING UP THE FINANCES TO HR

When I came into talent management and DEI (circa 2010), a lot of people described HR as being a bit of a secondary player in many corporations. In other words, people clearly valued the work being done, but the HR teams were often treated a bit as second-class citizens. Part of this was attributable to the fact that at the time, typically HR and DEI were not operational profit-line centers.

Another factor was that HR was not often provided with the full-scale company budgets. There are, of course, considerations as to why finance would often have to keep the bottom-line numbers somewhat confidential, particularly in private companies.

However, there can be a bit of a happy medium. One of the first things I've done in nearly all my assignments is to at least provide the top line analysis to my trusted other senior leaders, including HR.

Surprisingly, in nearly all instances in which I had done so, HR indicated that this was actually the first time that they had been afforded a look at the detailed numbers.

For at least a top line analysis, I could not see the harm and frankly found that this allowed people to be even more engaged because (a) they clearly felt more like a part of the senior management team, and (b) they could also somewhat see the results of the issues that were being discussed and jointly being agreed upon.

So, to me at least, including talent management/DEI/HR senior executives in at least some of the company financials is always a good thing to do. More informed decisions can be made thereby, and having more engaged senior managers is a wonderful by-product of this.

As a CFO, I totally understand the need for confidentiality, and some numbers likely should never be shared (except perhaps with the CEO). I am happy to say that when bringing all parties into the financial and budgetary discussions, it always produced better overall financial results.

24

Review of Lesson Learned

Include DEI/HR Senior Executives in Financial Decision-Making

There are, of course, numerous areas of finance that need to remain confidential for various reasons. However, I have found that including senior DEI/ HR managers in at least some of the financial decision-making can provide significant benefits. One is a higher sense of engagement when being provided with the data for the first time. In turn, this can create even better financial planning and budgeting for the future. This is something that I would recommend and have benefited from in the past where we have been able to actually implement it.

Career #4

COO/DEI

LESSON 25

Support Middle Management

Story #25

THE MIDDLE-MANAGEMENT DILEMMA

Understanding the middle-manager dilemma, as I call it, is a key consideration in evaluating the progress (or the lack thereof) that often occurs with respect to new DEI initiatives.

As perhaps we all know, no major new DEI initiative is likely to succeed within an organization unless the topmost senior C-suite executives sign off on it. Usually, this means the CEO as well. However, this often isn't enough. The CEO and the other senior C-suite executives need to then champion the initiative for it to actually gain some traction.

In the cases in which we are lucky enough to obtain both C-suite/CEO full buy-in and further championing, why do the initiatives still often fail?

In my experience, it isn't so much that the rest of the company—middle management, in particular—has an issue with the DEI initiative or doesn't believe in it (although that can, of course, sometimes be the case). I say it is rather a problem of what our middle managers are typically being asked to do. They begin with a tremendous number of duties and responsibilities. Then, as companies begin to further consolidate, flatten the curve, and embark on major new merger and acquisition initiatives, the duties being asked of middle managers often double and triple.

As we all know, a truly responsible DEI initiative requires a lot of work by many, continuous monitoring, and follow-up.

So guess what? Something has to give. And, unfortunately, as we all have often seen in the past, that something is the full-scale push for the new DEI initiative(s).

Again, I want to indicate that in my professional experience, it is not that the middle managers are actually against the DEI initiative. No, it's just that they are too buried to know what to prioritize and when and how.

So, what can be done?

First, I think a clear direction is necessary (for example, "This DEI initiative is critical, important, and needs to be implemented"). We need direction from the top. If we don't allow for more space, more time, and prioritizations that can change, how can middle managers suddenly produce these additional hours out of the air, so to speak, when they don't exist?

We have to help our middle managers: more people, more budgets, and reprioritizations. That is, at least, the beginning of better solutions, as I have found in the companies with which I have worked.

Review of Lesson Learned

Support Your Middle Managers

For any key DEI initiative to have traction, it must begin with the full-scale support of the topmost senior C-suite leaders, the CEO in particular. Then it must be actively, continuously supported by full C-suite management. When we get down to middle management, unless we support and give direction to them, all too often the major DEI initiative(s) will become bogged down and lost in the shuffle. It is our responsibility as key C-suite leadership executives to make sure that we create a viable means for our middle managers to support these initiatives timewise, budgetwise, and monetarily. The chances of a successful DEI initiative will then increase exponentially.

WORKBOOK

CAREER #4 LESSONS (21–25)

Themes: DEI Investment, Patience, Cultural Disconnect, Engagement, Middle Managers

Question 1: Have you ever been involved in a major DEI initiative? How was it supported? Was it relatively successful, and, if not, what do you think could have been done better?

_____

_____

_____

_____

_____

_____

Question 2: Have you ever worked in a company in which your US operations were distinct from the foreign corporate C-suite executive leadership? If so, did you experience, or were you aware of, any major cultural disconnects?

_____

_____

_____

_____

_____

Question 3: What has been your experience working with middle managers? Do you find that they are generally overworked and overburdened? Do you feel they have been appropriately supported?

_____

_____

_____

_____

_____

Career #5

Introduction
EXECUTIVE COACHING

- Work with Your Best People to Help Them, Including Introverted Leaders

- Celebrate Your Corporate Entrepreneurs

- Learning Never Stops

- Diversity of Experience in C-Suite Leadership Does Truly Matter

- It All Begins with Listening

Career #5

EXECUTIVE COACHING

LESSON 26

*Work with Your Best People to Help
Them, Including Introverted Leaders*

Story #26

WORK WITH YOUR BEST PEOPLE
TO HELP THEM

After having been a mentor and informal coach throughout most of my career(s), at the suggestion of a very special mentor I also entered into formal executive coaching around 2010.

This field has been and continues to be extremely rewarding for me in that, with my many experiences and careers, I am able to engage and coach clients from a wide range of disciplines and specialties. Nothing matches the joy of helping others find their way, take their next steps, create a strategy, and/or watching logic emerge.

It is truly a very wonderful experience to try and help others in this way.

I have been lucky enough to work with all sorts of candidates on all sorts of issues in multiple areas:

- Individual career transition

- Leadership development and life coaching

- Corporate C-suite leadership

- Talent management and retention coaching

- Shifts from corporate America to entrepreneurship

- Targeted executive coaching in sales, finance, health care, and handling of sexual harassment issues

Another group that I have also enjoyed working with is introverted candidates, helping them navigate how they approach their work—and their lives, for that matter.

What I have found most helpful for these candidates is to try and follow a two-track coaching scenario. In other words, we are typically focused on whatever their immediate need is (for example, their next job, advancement, promotion, etc.).

We need to also try to measure progress being made in terms of how they are dealing with their basic more introverted natures. In other words, we try to track their progress together and discuss how they have made some inroads in trying to be more comfortable—for example, in terms of networking and outreaches.

I have many examples that I could cite here, but one in particular went as follows: The candidate was extremely introverted (by their own definition), but the situation was compounded by the fact that they had just come out of a very, very tough work environment. To say that they also felt quite beaten down by their recent work experiences would not be a stretch. In fact, it was even quite physically apparent in the beginning.

So, the first (and in my humble opinion, most important) step is building that trust together. This took a little time, but we were able to do so.

Next was helping the candidate consider their next steps, how to strategize, what materials to prepare, and, most importantly, whom to meet to pursue their goals.

We created plans and strategies together and a grid to measure, and we made sure to go at the pace with which the candidate felt comfortable.

Ultimately, this led to a very good consulting position for the candidate, who began to feel reenergized and, little by little, more involved in talking and meeting with others.

After a while, the candidate, who continued on with me after securing their position, began to share that they had a number of ideas about the company. They thought the CEO might be interested in hearing about them. They expressed their hope that one day the CEO might recognize what these might be from their direct reports.

I startled my candidate a bit, I think, by saying, "Well, now you have been there for [x number of months], you have made valuable contributions, and with your past great experience have some new and interesting ideas that the CEO might not be aware of. So why don't you try and set up a meeting with the CEO yourself, making sure not to step on anyone's toes, and just let them know your thoughts?"

At first, dead silence. But as we talked it through, my candidate started to build up their confidence in being able to do so. Bottom line, the candidate did meet with the CEO, who was quite intrigued by the candidate's comments. Equally as important, it was a huge boost for this relatively introverted business leader. I could truly feel their joy in reaching the point at which they'd arrived, given where they had started.

I am not sure an executive coach could ask for a more rewarding experience.

26

Review of Lesson Learned

Work with Your Best People To Help Them, Including Introverted Leaders

Many times, your most capable people have other areas about which they are personally concerned. When it comes to introversion, as an example, take the time to help the person achieve not only the corporate goals that will help everyone, but also some of their own personal goals. In the end, this will only help them be even better key C-suite leaders—for you and for the company.

Career #5

EXECUTIVE COACHING

LESSON 27
Celebrate Your Corporate Entrepreneurs

Story #27

ENCOURAGE YOUR CORPORATE ENTREPRENEURS

Another area that I am seeing a number of candidates pursue these days is making the shift from corporate America to a more entrepreneurial arena.

This is true for a number of reasons: the need to spread one's wings, the need to try something new and different, being one's own boss, economics, excitement, and so on.

Here, I suggest considering a couple of key items. First, from the corporate perspective, wherever feasible, I always encourage my corporate clients to try and create incubator business opportunities and corporate disruption opportunities. This is an incredibly important part of helping make sure that companies continue to remain on the cutting edge when it comes to new innovation and strategies for growth. Of course, there are many dilemmas that may arise, but, rest assured, if structured correctly, these approaches can be extremely helpful.

Next, I suggest that companies identify, earlier rather than later, those employees who have a knack for and/or a strong interest in this type of work. When the company does so, it can create the opportunity internally and realize the benefit of not losing a very insightful mind sometime in the future.

Third, and this I have seen a lot, if the employee does, in fact, leave to try this new, more entrepreneurial route, most companies do not seem happy with the loss and tend to focus primarily on that aspect.

What I suggest is the much better approach of celebrating the employee and their new endeavor. Wish them the very, very best. And, who knows, they may even create something really amazing and bring it back to you as a potential customer or strategic partner!

27

Review of Lesson Learned

Celebrate Your Corporate Entrepreneurs

The shift from corporate America to potential entrepreneurship is palpable. It is happening more and more every day. Companies should first try to foster small internal incubators to encourage entrepreneurship (and even corporate disruption) where possible. They should next make sure to know their best-suited internal candidates and give them the leeway to succeed. Finally, if the urge is so strong that some candidates leave, rather than being unhappy about it, celebrate it…and them. Not only is it a better thing to do, but it may in fact subsequently pay back some huge new dividends.

Career #5

EXECUTIVE COACHING

LESSON 28

Learning Never Stops

Story #28

COACHING, LIKE LEARNING, NEVER STOPS

Another area that has been very delightful for me to experience in this past decade as an executive coach is the ability to continue on with many of my coaching clients, even as they progress and move into new areas of management.

For example, many of the candidates with whom I initially work come into the process in search of their next job or career transition. Strategies, networking, interview preparation, etc.—all of these are really important here.

When the candidate successfully lands a position, it is a pleasure to see that they often would like to continue on in our executive coaching together. The cadence, of course, now typically shifts. It is not as critical to meet weekly, as it was during the career-transition phase.

Here, after some initial onboarding coaching, the topic(s) often shift to advancement within the new entity, leadership development, corporate communications, strategic and financial business consulting, and the like.

Of course, there are often some more personal issues, such as advancing high-potential women leaders, DEI, change management, emotional intelligence, etc.

As I said, it is incredibly rewarding to me as an executive coach to be able to try and assist in these new areas as part of the continuing development and growth of emerging leaders.

So, what is the key leadership lesson for C-suite leaders?

I suggest that, as these candidates have shown, learning actually never stops. There are always new issues and areas to grow into and learn about. C-suite leaders are wise to remember that—both for ourselves and certainly in encouraging our own workforce. The dividends can be extremely meaningful.

28

Review of Lesson Learned

Learning Never Stops

C-suite leaders can learn from what many job candidates have exhibited. In other words, just because candidates have learned and navigated the whole job-search arena and have now successfully landed a position, this doesn't necessarily mean that they stop there. They shift their executive-coaching focus to the next level of needs, advancement, and overall leadership learning. This is a good, key C-suite leadership lesson for all of us to remember as well, not only as C-suite leaders, but as a strong imperative to encourage within our own organizations.

Career #5

EXECUTIVE COACHING

LESSON 29

Diversity of Experience in C-Suite Leadership Does Truly Matter

Story #29

DIVERSITY OF EXPERIENCE IN THE C-SUITE DOES REALLY MATTER

As I have demonstrated through discussing my five careers (and pre-career), each was quite different. Still, overall, there were many great C-suite leadership lessons to be learned from each and every one of them. Clearly, I know that I have greatly benefited from having had those various different corporate and business experiences.

In executive coaching, I believe that the same principle applies. In other words, the more business and leadership experience a coach has had, the more the additional perspectives learned and new areas explored, all combine to create a more diverse or well-rounded coach.

Some might counsel that it is best to focus on one area or one expertise, but a more successful approach is actually to be able to speak to a subject from personal experience and varying perspectives.

My own work as an executive coach, as I mentioned earlier, encompasses career transition, life coaching, and corporate leadership development coaching as its main pillars. But it also includes DEI coaching, numerous personal areas, and some very specialized areas (for example, training in handling sexual harassment issues).

Added to the mix, as an attorney I am often involved as an executive coach in reviewing contracts and negotiating executive compensation packages and the like. And as a CFO, I analyze various merger and acquisition scenarios, create business plans, etc. Clearly, I love the variety of the work.

Even more importantly, from the client/candidate perspective, my being at least generally familiar with many additional areas tends to give them a great deal of comfort.

Of course, knowing when to say that x is an area that I really don't know much about and requires hiring a better expert is critically important too!

So what is my suggested key C-suite leadership lesson here? I say that, whenever possible, be sure to surround yourself with people who have worn multiple hats, have seen several different facets of your business, and, ideally, have often had similar experiences.

All too often, especially in the senior-talent management area, I tend to see generalists being a bit frowned upon. On the contrary, the very depth of their incredible array of experiences can bring much needed value to the C-suite.

Yes, the diversity of experience can truly make a difference.

Review of Lesson Learned

Diversity of Experience in C-Suite Leadership Does Truly Matter

As the world grows smaller, and more corporations are international and multifaceted, now more than ever diversity of experience can truly make a difference. When C-suite leaders can take a broader view, a more encompassing view, and, ideally, even have real-life examples that they can cite in a particular area or domain, it is incredibly helpful. Also, understanding the potential impact of a certain set of actions across multiple domains is an invaluable perspective.

Career #5

EXECUTIVE COACHING

LESSON 30

It All Begins with Listening

Story #30

IT ALL BEGINS WITH LISTENING

In this last key C-suite leadership lesson, I would like to focus on one initial key variable: it all begins with listening.

A key issue that has arisen (especially in the workplace) is that many people are simply unable to listen to others. I see this all the time. In fact, it is often as though some people are already planning their responses / rejoinders before they have even heard what the other person has to say. This is not a very productive conversation, not only in the personal sphere, but absolutely in the business realm. People end up talking over one another, not catching what the other person is actually trying to say. Not to mention how disrespected the other person then often typically feels. It is not a very good model for making progress, creating better understanding, and / or solving a problem!

I have personally seen this countless times in corporate America, in personal conversations, and in many places.

The approach I have always taken in both executive coaching and, hopefully, in my own personal life, is to begin with listening. And I mean *really* listening—with an open mind, no prejudgment, and no preconditioned viewpoints. Think first about what the candidate is saying, why it matters to them, and what message is being conveyed.

Only then can you really begin the process of truly trying to help the candidate move forward with whatever they are seeking to do next.

The same applies in business. If someone has already made up their mind and is therefore not actually hearing the other side, the prognosis for a meaningful solution becomes quite diminished.

As C-suite leaders, I say that this lesson is particularly strong. Always, always begin by truly trying to understand what the other person is saying. Even if they are fundamentally on the other side of an issue, you might actually learn something very meaningful. And, at a minimum, you will be much more likely to produce a real solution that will work for both sides.

30

Review of Lesson Learned

It All Begins with Listening

Just as with executive coaching, it is imperative for key C-suite leaders to begin tackling really meaningful problems by first listening with an open mind. Too often, we have already drawn lines in the sand, predetermined that another particular point of view is not meaningful, etc. And, of course, sometimes that can be the case. But sometimes it is not. We must start by truly listening to see what solutions are being proposed. In this way, it is far more likely that a true—and lasting—solution will be found.

WORKBOOK

CAREER #5 LESSONS (26–30)

Themes: Introspective Leadership, Corporate Entrepreneurs, Always Learning, Diversity of Experience, Listening

Question 1: Has your company fostered a sense of internal entrepreneurship? If not, what are some areas that you think would be fruitful to pursue?

_____

_____

_____

_____

_____

_____

_____

Question 2: In your experience, do you feel you have learned more from senior leaders who have one key expertise, or from senior leaders who have more broad/diversified experience? What key experiences do you bring to your leadership role and team?

_____

_____

_____

_____

_____

_____

_____

_____

_____

_____

_____

Question 3: Recall a situation(s) in which leaders were seemingly talking AT one another, rather than TO one another? What complications did this cause, and what recommendations do you have for a more productive outcome?

_____

_____

_____

_____

_____

_____

_____

_____

_____

_____

_____

_____

_____

ASH VARMA
NYC

Let's Connect

Find out more about Ash Varma, Esq.
at the following links!

Official Website: ashvarmanyc.com

Email: ash@ashvarmanyc.com

LinkedIn: linkedin.com/in/ashvarmanyc/